DATE DUE

DEMCO 38-296

LITHIUM: WHAT YOU SHOULD KNOW

Lithium is a substance used to treat illnesses such as ADD/ADHD and bipolar disorder.

LITHIUM:
WHAT YOU SHOULD KNOW

Daniel Eshom

THE ROSEN PUBLISHING GROUP, INC.
NEW YORK

for Opus

The people pictured in this book are only models. They in no way practice or endorse the activities illustrated. Captions serve only to explain the subjects of photographs and do not in any way imply a connection between the real-life models and the staged situations.

Published in 1999 by The Rosen Publishing Group, Inc.
29 East 21st Street, New York, NY 10010

Copyright © 1999 by The Rosen Publishing Group, Inc.

Library of Congress Cataloging-in-Publication Data

Eshom, Daniel.
    Lithium: what you should know / Daniel Eshom
    p.   cm. — (The Drug Abuse Prevention Library)
    Includes bibliographical references and index.
    Summary: Describes the nature and effects of lithium, how it is used to treat mood disorders and ADD, and alternative forms of treatment.
    ISBN 0-8239-2828-4
      1. Lithium—Therapeutic use—Juvenile Literature. 2. Manic-depressive illness—Chemotherapy—Juvenile literature. 3. Manic-depressive illness in adolescence—Chemotherapy—Juvenile literature. 4. Attention-deficit hyperactivity disorder—Chemotherapy—Juvenile literature. [1. Lithium. 2. Manic-depressive illness. 3. Mental illness. 4. Attention-deficit hyperactivity disorder.] I. Title. II. Series.
    RC483.5.L5E83 1999
    616.89'18—dc21   98-40924
                                                                                  CIP
                                                                                   AC

Manufactured in the United States of America

Contents

Introduction

Lately Simon felt as if he were two people inside the same body. Two very different people.

Many mornings, he woke to a sinking feeling in the pit of his stomach. Just the thought of getting up, showering, and walking to school totally exhausted him. He wished he could stay in his room, keep his eyes closed, and not talk to anyone. But Simon would eventually force his body upright, taking deep breaths, eyes squeezed shut, trying not to cry. His arms and legs felt leaden and sluggish. He imagined they had been replaced overnight by heavy, waterlogged bath towels. Not even the thought of basketball practice beginning in a few weeks made him feel better.

Simon knew that what he was feeling was some sort of heavy depression. "The blues," his mom would call it. But what he didn't know—and what made these mornings especially frustrating and frightening—was the source of his mood. As far as he could see, he had no reason to be depressed. Simon had no physical injuries. No great tragedies had happened to him or his family, at least not since his favorite aunt died of cancer a few years ago. He had a few really close friends with whom he could talk about anything and, except for algebra, he actually enjoyed his classes—not that he would ever admit it to his mom. So what was making him feel this way?

Then there was the flip side, the times Simon imagined that the other "person" in his body was emerging. These times were just as exhausting and made him feel even more out of control. Simon would start to feel antsy and anxious, as if something were about to happen. His thoughts raced through his head, and words flew from his mouth. He couldn't stand to sit still and study, even if he had a test the next day. Because the next day always seemed too far away; today he wanted to move, to laugh, to talk. Simon once went three days without sleeping.

Eventually, though, he always fell back into the depression he was in before, when all he wanted was to be alone. With each swing, Simon's low periods dropped even lower, and his

8 | *highs grew to more and more frenzied heights, full of increasingly reckless episodes. Simon's mom, worried and unable to figure out what was causing his extreme mood swings, took him to the family doctor. After a careful, in-depth physical exam that showed nothing unusual, the doctor handed Simon pen and paper.*

"Maybe it would help if you took a few minutes to describe what you've been feeling lately," the doctor suggested.

Simon didn't bother taking a few minutes. He picked up the pen and quickly scrawled across the paper.

Holding it up to reveal a jagged series of sharp peaks, shaky lines, and deep valleys, he said, "This pretty much sums up my moods. I can't control myself. High and low, up and down. It never stops. I can't tell you how I'll feel from one day to the next, sometimes even from one hour to the next. I don't understand it."

Have you ever felt like Simon? Do you know anyone whose behavior matches Simon's drawing?

The feelings Simon describes are not uncommon. Millions of Americans feel this way. They are suffering from a psychological disorder marked by severe changes in mood between elation, or high spirits, and heavy depression. In one phase, they may **9** feel agitated or irritable and can become hyperactive, getting by with little sleep; in the next, they may experience deep sadness, inactivity, difficulty in concentrating, a loss of appetite, feelings of hopelessness, and sometimes thoughts of suicide. The swings from one extreme to the other are very exhausting and can leave one feeling absolutely helpless. As you can see from Simon's situation, living with a mood disorder is both frightening and frustrating. Also, because it's difficult to know how to help—or even to know what to expect from —someone like Simon, mood disorders take a heavy toll on friends and family.

Some teens and adults find that talking to a therapist or psychiatrist helps a lot. But others find they need more help. That's when they are given a medication, or a psychiatric drug. Psychiatric drugs are legal (approved by the United States Food and Drug Administration) mind-altering drugs prescribed by doctors. Today, psychiatric drugs allow us to treat depression, relieve anxiety, and help solve a wide variety of health problems.

Lithium is one of these medications. It is the most widely prescribed drug for mood and behavior problems. It is also

10 among the most misunderstood. There are really no other medications like lithium. It is not an antidepressant, which stimulates the chemicals in the brain and helps people who are diagnosed as clinically depressed. You're probably familiar with Prozac, which is the most widely prescribed anti-depressant. Nor is lithium a barbiturate, or sedative, for helping extremely anxious or even hysterical patients.

Lithium is actually a mood stabilizer, a sort of combination of these two types of medication. Medical doctors prescribe it for people having difficulties similar to Simon's. Although it is occasionally pre-scribed for children under twelve, the main medical purpose for lithium is to help sta-bilize uncontrollable moods and behaviors in older teens and adults.

This book will neither condemn nor endorse this medication. Instead, it will simply give you the whole scoop on lithium: what it is, and the various reasons for taking it. Along the way, you'll meet several other teens like Simon and learn all about their different experiences with mood disorders, family disruptions, and lithium.

"I can't tell you how I'll feel from one day to the next. High and low, up and down." Millions of Americans suffer from bipolar disorder, marked by severe changes in mood.

In addition to being an ingredient in psychiatric drugs, lithium is used to make tennis rackets, support skyscrapers, and build spacecraft.

CHAPTER 1

What Is Lithium?

*O*n Nirvana's massively successful and critically acclaimed punk-rock album *Nevermind*, the late Kurt Cobain sings with sadness and anger about how it feels to be on lithium. But on television, in novels, and at the movies, you may have noticed how lithium is often referred to as a "miracle" drug that supposedly erases all negative or sad feelings. And many people associate it closely with mental hospitals and psychiatric wards. Lots of completely different messages reach us about lithium—which ones are accurate?

On top of all that, you might have heard about how NASA considers lithium one of its most valuable ingredients in designing new spacecraft. Maybe you've watched the

14 lifeguard at the pool adding a silvery liquid to the chlorinated water, and you're sure she said it was called "lithium." And what's the deal with those lithium batteries?

The things we hear about lithium in our culture are vague and very mixed. Are all of these "lithiums" the same lithium? It doesn't seem to make any sense.

So what are the facts? What exactly is lithium? Where does it come from? What is it for?

Let's start at the beginning.

First things first: lithium was not created in a laboratory. It is an all-natural metal, one of the many chemical elements that make up the ingredients of our planet. Lithium carbonate is the lightest solid element on Earth—it weighs less than half as much as the air we breathe. At the same time, it is incredibly strong and resilient. Because of lithium's seemingly miraculous flexibility, it is used to build space shuttles, support skyscrapers, enliven golf balls, kill algae in swimming pools, strengthen glass, supply the power in wristwatch batteries, and much more.

Lithium as a Drug

Lithium was actually introduced into psychiatry by accident. In 1949, an Australian

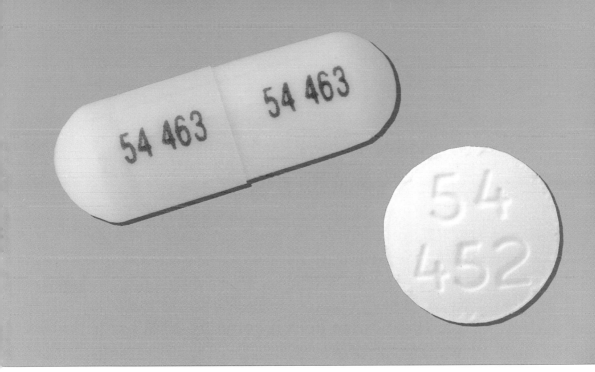

Lithium is available in capsules, tablets, and liquid form.

physicist named John Cade was testing his hypothesis that the acid (or carbonate) in lithium would somehow cause excited behavior in animals. He was in for a big surprise: When Cade injected the lithium into guinea pigs, they became quite calm and unresponsive. When he poked at them, they did not scamper away. And when he put them on their backs, instead of trying to quickly scramble back onto their feet, the typically jittery guinea pigs just lay quietly.

So Cade's hypothesis was turned completely inside out. It seemed at this point that lithium performed as a sedative, or a calming drug.

Cade then conducted similar tests on

16 | people, half of whom had been diagnosed as manic, or extremely high-strung and energetic, and the other half as depressed, exhibiting unusually low energy levels. Based on his results from the guinea pig experiments, Cade was not surprised to find that the lithium injections helped only the manic half of the human test group. The surprise came from how very dramatically these patients improved: as with the guinea pigs, their tense and edgy tendencies completely disappeared. No other drug had proved so effective in treating jittery and nervous symptoms.

These tests were performed illegally, without the knowledge or approval of Australia's government. As a result of this, lithium was not recognized as an acceptable medication in the United States until 1970, when it was finally approved by the Food and Drug Administration. This approval came after several years of legal experiments with lithium, which yielded discoveries similar to Cade's, with one significant exception: scientists found that, in most cases, lithium helped stabilize both manic and depressive symptoms.

Today, lithium carbonate has become the drug most commonly prescribed to treat people suffering from illnesses that

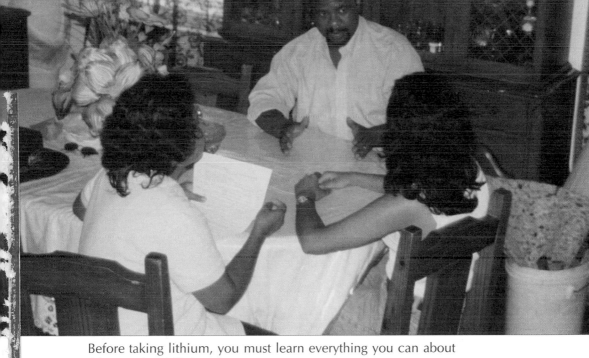

Before taking lithium, you must learn everything you can about this mood-stabilizing drug.

involve mania, hyperactivity, and difficulty controlling moods and feelings. Although most of these people are adults, lithium is also prescribed for children and teenagers. When a person is prescribed a lithium medication, he or she takes it every day. There are many different brand names for lithium—including Lithotabs, Lithane, Lithizine, Cibalith, and Duralith—and they are available in capsule, tablet, and liquid form. The pills are usually white or peach colored, and the syrups are clear.

If you or someone you know is facing the decision of whether to begin taking lithium, it will make things safer and easier if you know as much as possible about it. Even though you may not be the one actually on

Talking to your doctor can help answer your questions about lithium.

the medication, lithium becomes a critical ingredient in your life the moment a close friend or loved one begins taking it. Because it is a very serious decision, it is very important to get all of the facts. The following chapters discuss the specific problems that lithium treatment may or may not help solve, as well as the issues and questions that should be considered.

CHAPTER 2

Lithium and Mood Disorders

Kim's story below illustrates how mood disorders can affect an entire family.

At my house these days, you never know what to expect. It feels like I'm on a roller coaster, going up and down, but I'm really not. It's my mom.

Every afternoon, while I'm making a snack or listening to music, I worry about what might happen in the evening. I picture Mom in one of the several moods she's constantly stepping into and then shedding all of a sudden, without any warning or apparent reason . . .

Standing in the kitchen with a carton of milk in her hand, red-faced, screaming at the top of her lungs at me and my sister about the expiration date . . . Or on the telephone, possibly that

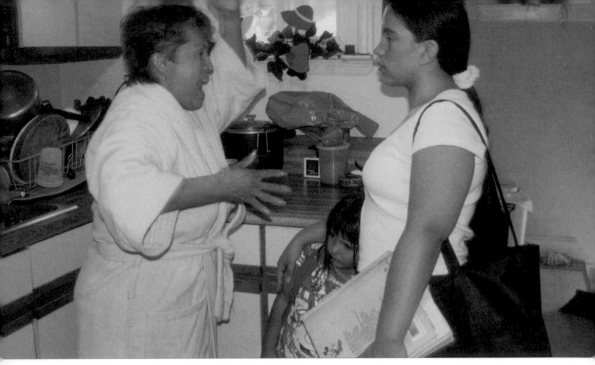

It is painful and frightening to live with a parent who has a mood disorder. It's common to have feelings of guilt and frustration.

same night, talking super-fast and nonstop, her hands cutting frantically through the air as she explains herself, laughing really loudly and shouting out cusswords, which she almost never does . . . And then there is the mood she seems to be in most often lately, the one that worries me the most—silent, her bedroom door shut, unable even to talk to us. Whenever that happens, we get so scared that we have to go in to check on her. Her eyes, when she looks up at me, are terrified. It's very scary to see your mom looking so helpless.

Some days she comes home from work and seems fine—she always tells us how sorry she is about how she's been acting, saying she sometimes just can't control her feelings. On
those nights, I feel like we're a normal family—

my brother and I do homework, and Mom pays
bills, clips coupons from the newspaper, or reads
a book.

Sooner or later, though, it always happens
again. I always have this terrible feeling that
maybe I'm doing something wrong, that maybe
it's my fault whenever my mom feels so sad, or
gets so angry, or seems really edgy and out of
control, as if she just drank a whole gallon of
coffee or something.

I worry about her while I'm at school, won-
dering what I can do to make her feel better. I
don't dare bring any of my friends home for
fear she might do something embarrassing. I
know that sounds terrible, but it's true. Don't
think it doesn't make me feel like a total jerk
for saying all of this, because it does.

I wish there was some way to help her.

Every day we experience different feelings
and moods. Life is all about reacting to our
surroundings and to the various events—
good and bad—that shape each day.
Feeling down is a typical reaction when sad
or difficult things happen. When you run
into a good friend you haven't seen in a
while, you probably feel upbeat and happy.
In the moments just before a big test for
which you spent a lot of time studying, you
may feel a little anxious. We can usually

Disordered? Or Just a Very Bad Day?

Bipolar disorder is an ongoing, chronic difficulty. Just having a really terrible day or two—maybe right on the heels of a couple of truly fantastic days—then taking your problems out on others by yelling, and feeling very guilty about it afterward, does not necessarily mean you have a mood disorder.

Since it is natural to have different moods and feelings from day to day, it's very easy to read about bipolar disorder and identify with some of the symptoms and feelings. In some cases there may be something real and beneficial to this identification. Reading this book can lead to support, understanding, and recovery. But many times we are simply worrying about having feelings that are perfectly natural and healthy.

identify the things that cause our moods. **23**
Many people find that life is usually
happier and more satisfying, for ourselves
as well as for our families and friends, when
we try to maintain a balance between our
high and low moods. Sometimes the
balance comes naturally; other times it can
be difficult.

For some people, this emotional balance
is extremely difficult, even impossible, to
maintain. These people suffer from a type
of medical illness called an affective disorder, or a mood disorder, and they have little
or no control over their changing moods.
Bipolar disorder is a type of ongoing mood
disorder that involves marked changes in a
person's mood between extreme elation or
happiness and severe depression. The
symptoms Kim described in her mother's
behavior are indications of bipolar disorder. You may have heard this type of
problem described as manic depression,
which is another term for bipolar disorder.

The periods of elation are known as
mania. During the mania phase, a person
often feels very agitated, sometimes hyperactive, and gets by with very little or no sleep.
Sometimes he or she seems unusually ecsta-
tic and even silly. The manic person is often
very distractible, talks very fast, changes

24 topics abruptly, and cannot be interrupted. Other times, the person may act uncharacteristically irritable and grumpy. He or she may also engage in risky behavior, such as sexual promiscuity or getting into fistfights.

In combination with these "highs" are the "lows"—the periods of depression. The depressive symptoms include persistent feelings of sadness, frequent crying, and a loss of enjoyment and interest in favorite activities. He or she may also have some of the following symptoms:

- Low energy level
- Difficulty in concentrating
- Unusual sleeping patterns such as oversleeping or trouble sleeping at all
- Eating too much or too little
- Frequent complaints of illnesses such as headaches or stomachaches
- Feelings of guilt, worthlessness, or ugliness
- Suicidal thoughts

Bipolar disorder usually starts in adult life, between the ages of twenty and thirty-five, but it also occurs in teenagers. There are various ways bipolar disorder can affect teens in particular.

Brian is fourteen. He has always been

aggressive and very active. By the time he started school, he had already been seen by a pediatric psychiatrist for his tantrums and reckless behavior. Luckily, he had not gotten into too much trouble, until now.

A week ago Brian just took off. Mad at his dad for not letting him go to his friend Doug's house after dinner, Brian threw a plate at him and ran away on foot. A week later, after a major search, the police called saying they had found him. According to their reports, he had broken into two houses and stolen cigarettes and bottles of liquor. His friend Doug, who was with Brian the first few days hiding out at a campground on the outskirts of town, went to the police because Brian was beginning to really scare him. Brian was running around the camp all night long, shouting and screaming songs from a CD he had. When the police found him, Brian acted very friendly and outgoing, talking a mile a minute, and wanting them to listen to his CD. Then he took off into the woods. It took the police another hour to find him. They had to place him under arrest.

After staying home from school for a couple of days, Brian slowly came back to his old self, but he was deeply depressed. He couldn't understand why he had done these things. No one else could, either.

26 | *Brian is on probation for the next three years, and some of his old friends' parents still won't let their children hang out with him.*

Katie is thirteen years old. She had been feeling depressed for about six months. She wasn't suicidal, but she just sort of sat around in her room all the time, getting increasingly irritable. Katie began doing much worse in school than before. By not returning phone calls and ignoring people at school, she started letting a lot of her friendships go, and the only thing that still got her excited was when her older sister came home for visits from college in North Carolina.

Over the last few days Katie finally started to come out of her slump. She started calling old friends, began playing the piano again for the first time in over half a year, and even seemed more interested in her schoolwork. It was last Friday when Katie's parents noticed that she was giggling a lot, virtually nonstop. She called about ten friends and invited them over. They were playing "truth or dare" in her bedroom, and Katie started giggling really loudly, coming up with new rules, and making all sorts of jokes, only a few of which were funny. Katie thought they were all funny. She put socks on her ears and started dancing around the room. Her friends didn't think it

The combination of inconsistent symptoms and moods can be very frightening. If you feel this way, talk to someone you trust who can help you.

was funny. Katie got mad all of a sudden and told them to go home.

The whole weekend was rough. Her parents were awakened to piano playing throughout the night, and every hour or so Katie would zoom into their bedroom to tell them something she had forgotten. What she said was so mixed up with giggling and gasping, that they couldn't understand her. That Monday, the principal called her dad at his office to have him pick her up. The principal said she was "disrupting the whole class and acting like a two-year-old." Katie kept laughing, he said, but no one else was.

Katie's mother took a two-week leave from work to stay at home with her and make sure she didn't hurt herself. Eventually she slowed

28 | *down and returned to the depressed state she had been in for the last six months. It took months before her old friends would have anything to do with her.*

Todd, fourteen, was not an indoors kind of guy. He was constantly outside, building something, trying to catch snakes, playing baseball in the summer, soccer in the fall, and hockey in the winter. He was also turning out to be a real asset on his father's boat. The lobster season before last year's, the other fishermen at the wharf often commented on what a fine young man Todd was becoming.

About a year ago, Todd had an episode of ongoing depression in which he did not want to do any sports at all and just sat around at home. He gained ten pounds and spent most of his time in the family room playing video games. He was barely passing in school, and his brothers were starting to get really annoyed at how he was always just lying around doing nothing. The only time he showed any energy or emotion was when he was angry, yelling at his family to leave him alone. He seemed to enjoy slamming doors and shouting at the top of his voice, because he started to do these things more and more often, especially once he realized how much it bothered his mom.

When his brothers finally got him to go out

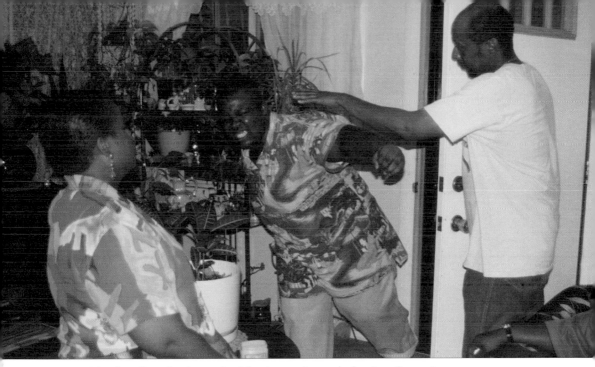
Bipolar disorder is marked by inconsistent behavior. Sometimes this can turn violent.

with them and ride the family's four-wheeler dune buggy, he crashed it into a tree. He didn't seem to worry about it all. His older brother even told Todd that it looked as if he had crashed it on purpose. Todd just shrugged. When his dad approached him about the accident, Todd got very angry, cursed at him, and walked off.

He started getting into fights at school. He started wearing only purple clothes. Why? Because he was "King." At first, Todd's family thought it was kind of a joke the way he treated everyone as if they were his subjects. Very quickly, it wasn't funny at all.

As you read about Brian, Katie, and Todd, it's easy to see how their friends and family could get very angry at them. Their behavior

30 is very frustrating and inconsiderate. This is often the way with mood disorders. The challenge for teens witnessing a family member's or friend's difficulties is remembering that this behavior is not a reflection on who the person really is. Once help is found, there's a good chance that things will get back to normal.

The bipolar-disordered person's highs may alternate with lows in intervals of weeks or even months. Or the person may feel both extremes at close to the same time. This combination of inconsistent symptoms can be very frightening, for the person suffering from them as well as for loved ones. They are especially frightening for someone like Kim, who doesn't understand what is happening to her mother, and wonders whether it might be her fault. Guilt and low self-esteem are common byproducts of severe mood disorders. It is very important to realize that bipolar disorder is nobody's fault. The only fault is not trying to get help.

Perhaps the most difficult part of dealing with mood disorders is the challenge of looking past all of the hurtful behavior and taking the steps toward diagnosis and treatment. First among these steps, when the periods of mania and

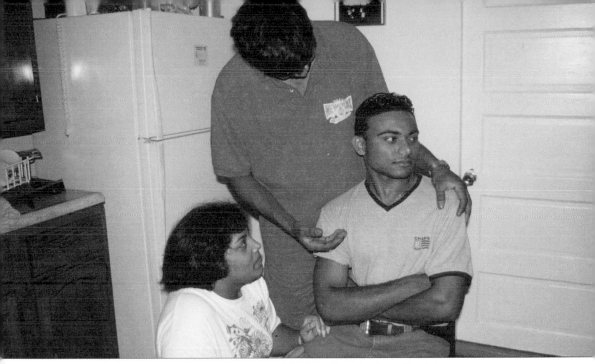

It is important to remember that bipolar disorder is nobody's fault. The only fault to be found is in not trying to get help.

depression are beginning to dominate a person's life (and the lives of his or her loved ones), is a visit to the family doctor. This way, the process of getting help can begin as quickly as possible.

Many teens and adults may respond angrily when approached about going to see a counselor and a doctor. Understandably, they may first perceive it as a punishment. Talking to them patiently and calmly may enable them to understand that this can help them feel more in control and better about themselves.

Treating Bipolar Disorder

Doctors are not sure whether bipolar disorder is a genetic disorder (a disorder that

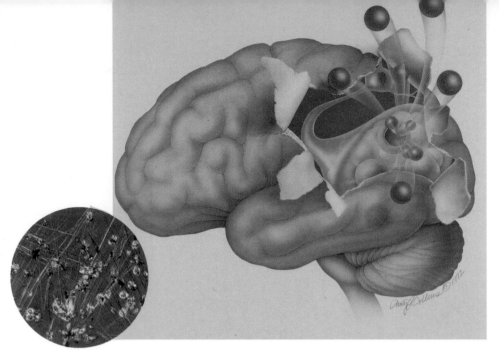

A dramatized diagram of the brain releasing neurotransmitters. To the left: a close-up of serotonin.

occurs in certain people because of biological traits passed on from their parents) or an illness that develops because of a person's particular environment and experiences. However, studies have found that children and teens with a manic-depressive parent have a higher chance of developing the illness themselves.

Many medical scientists believe that people who suffer from mood illnesses may have a chemical imbalance in the brain. The brain's message senders (neurotransmitters), particularly a chemical called serotonin, are just not doing their jobs very effectively.

As you have seen in the stories above, bipolar disorder can be very serious, or

even fatal, if steps are not taken to treat it.
Since both the manic and depressive symptoms are similar to those that occur in
people with other problems, such as drug
abuse, doctors are very careful in diagnos-
ing someone with bipolar disorder.

Alternatives to Medication

Before deciding to prescribe medication, a
doctor may first recommend a few steps
that often help ease the suffering of bipolar
disorder. For many people, a lifestyle
adjustment to accommodate these strate-
gies is the key to coping with their painful
bouts with mood swings.

Therapy: Regular visits, usually weekly
or biweekly, are made to a therapist or psychiatrist to talk about feelings and the
potential causes of manic or depressive
symptoms.

Change in diet: Establishing consistent
mealtimes, increasing the amount of fruits,
vegetables, and fibers in your diet, and
cutting back on sugar, processed foods,
and foods high in saturated fat can significantly improve your health, physically and
mentally. You might also ask your doctor
about which vitamins and herbal supple-
ments you should take.

A regular exercise program: A combination

34 of cardiovascular exercise, extensive muscle stretching, and tension-easing breathing exercises three or four times a week can make a big difference. Physical activity stimulates chemicals in the brain called endorphins, which act as natural antide-pressants and can help steady a person's mood.

Treating Bipolar Disorder with Lithium

Lithium carbonate, the drug most com-monly used to treat bipolar disorder, serves as a mood stabilizer. According to the National Alliance for the Mentally Ill, it has had a positive effect on 70 to 80 percent of the bipolar patients who have taken it.

Your family doctor may give you a phys-ical examination before starting lithium treatment. It is important that the bipolar patient's kidney and thyroid function, blood level, and blood-cell count be closely monitored before and during medication. Be sure to ask about each of these, espe-cially blood level, before you or a loved one begins lithium treatment. When blood level is too low, the manic and depressive symp-toms are usually not controlled at all. Also, since lithium is a particularly powerful and invasive drug, it is very important that the prescription schedule be strictly followed.

Taking too much lithium—taking it too frequently, or "double-dosing"—can result in
a very dangerous toxic blood condition and
can cause permanent damage to the central
nervous system.

Lithium and Pregnancy

A study was done in 1992 to measure the
effect of lithium on unborn babies. It was
found that mothers who took lithium
during pregnancy gave birth to babies with
a slightly higher risk of heart problems.
Also, birth weight was found to be significantly higher in the babies of mothers on
lithium. Although lithium is not a prohibited
medication during pregnancy, researchers
advise that expectant mothers' blood levels
be checked more frequently.

What Exactly Happens When You Take Lithium?

No one has figured out exactly what
lithium does to the body. The specific
actions lithium performs to prevent mood
swings are unknown, although it certainly
involves a combination of different actions.
Most researchers believe that much of
lithium's effect is on the entire central
nervous system, the mechanism that regu-
lates all body functions, including the

36 brain, spinal cord, and all nerve endings.

If the idea of regularly swallowing something that no one understands completely—in this case, a metal element mined from the earth—seems to you very strange and even dangerous, you're not alone. Many doctors and therapists are wary of the unknown properties of lithium and do not prescribe it for patients. On the other hand, lithium has been rated one of the most effective psychiatric drugs, and it remains by far the most popular treatment for bipolar disorder. Recently developed antidepressants, notably Prozac, have been shown to work wonders on depression, but do not control mania.

The Lithium Process

The first month on lithium medication is a period when the body adjusts to hosting a dominant new ingredient. Since two to three weeks may be required for lithium to begin having an effect on the manic portion of bipolar symptoms, doctors may also prescribe Haldol, a drug with quicker and more powerful "anti-manic" properties, in conjunction with lithium until the manic symptoms disappear. Also, many bipolar patients, at the beginning of lithium treatment, sink into a persistent depression

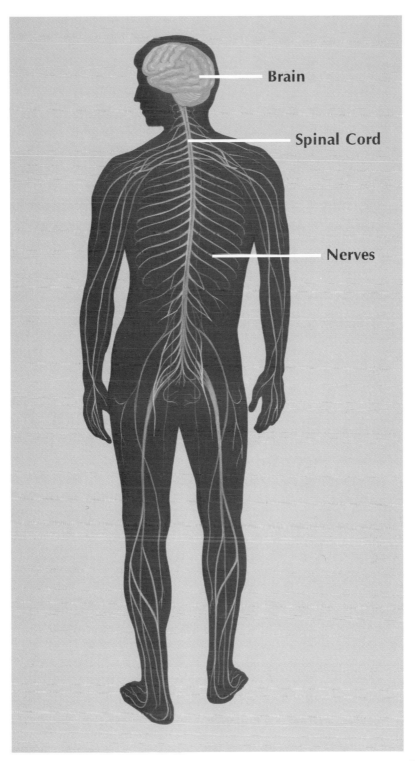

Brain

Spinal Cord

Nerves

The human nervous system.

38 marked by exhaustion and difficulty concentrating. Early side effects, which usually diminish over time, include loss of appetite, nausea, and mild diarrhea.

The average dosage of lithium for bipolar patients is about 300 milligrams, two to four times a day. It can be taken in capsules, tablets, or a syrup. If you experience side effects from lithium, you should notify your doctor promptly. These may include:

- Dizziness and hand tremors
- Weight gain
- Excessive sweating and body rashes
- Metallic taste in the mouth and persistent thirst
- Blurred vision

Some patients who benefit from lithium treatment are able to stop taking the medication after a period of time and avoid recurring manic-depressive symptoms. Others continue to take lithium for several years.

Kim (Part 2)

It looks like my family's roller-coaster ride might finally be ending.

Three months ago, when things were still really bad, my Uncle Jesse persuaded Mom to go see our family doctor. Mom was referred to a psychiatrist—a kind of doctor who, I found out, specializes in helping people through problems like we've been having.

Mom goes and talks about things with Dr. Swann every week. My sister and I have gone a couple of times, too. We learned all about my mom's bipolar disorder, and why her moods were constantly changing. And I finally got to talk out loud about how guilty and scared I always felt before Mom started getting help. It was such a relief to be able to explain my feelings.

Dr. Swann also prescribed for my mother a medication called Lithobid. It's supposed to steady her moods. She goes for tests every couple of weeks so the doctor can make sure the lithium isn't doing anything terrible to her body. I was worried at first that the drug would turn Mom into a completely different person, or make her sleep all the time, or act really "out of it" or something.

That hasn't happened at all. She's still totally Mom, just a lot less unpredictable.

CHAPTER 3

Lithium and ADD/ADHD

Grant, by all accounts, is an incredible teen. He's bright, articulate, and very funny. His teachers and friends say he's the life of the party, a one-man comedy act, and always the one full of great ideas. There's something very charismatic about him. Wherever Grant is, that's where you want to be.

Most of the time he does really well in school . . . except for the days when he forgets to hand in his homework because he simply "forgot to bring it." And there are the days when he goes home with every intention to study for a big test the next day, but forgets to take the necessary books home with him. His parents are frustrated, his teachers are angry, and Grant wishes everyone would just leave him alone!

Right now, Grant is sitting in his earth

science class, and Mr. Hampshire is saying something about the extreme temperatures found at the Earth's core, which triggers a thought about the thermometer in Grant's backyard, and suddenly he is thinking about how incredibly hot it is in the classroom and how he would like nothing better than to be in the shade in his backyard drinking a lemonade. That thought takes him to the weekend just another day away and how it would be a blast if he could have a bunch of friends over Friday night for a pool party. They could cook out on the grill. Thoughts of the grill lead to a bonfire at the reservoir once the evenings start getting longer. Suddenly, Mr. Hampshire is yelling at Grant again for not paying attention and disrupting the class.

So goes another day in the life of Grant. He sometimes feels that he never quite measures up.

Josie

Until my brother started taking his medication, this was the whole deal on drugs and my life: there was no deal.

The way I saw it, there were two basic types of drugs: There were the drugs you took when you were sick with the flu or a cold, of course. Then there were what I liked to call the "just-say-no" drugs. You know, the illegal drugs everybody's been warning you about nonstop since the

42 *third grade—pot, acid, cocaine, ecstasy, and all that stuff. It's always been cut- and-dried for me. Don't do them and you won't end up like my Uncle Randy, who's in prison for dealing, or like Kelly, who used to live upstairs from us until she overdosed on heroin last spring and died. She was seventeen. That's not going to happen to me. I want to go to college and move to San Francisco and work in graphic design. I don't want to alter my mind; I want to sharpen it.*

My little brother is a different story. Jeff is in fifth grade. He has always had a hard time in school because the teachers say they can't control him, that he doesn't pay attention. He usually gets low grades, and his teachers comment on his below-average performance.

Now, I can understand when they say he acts really hyper all the time—I know that better than anyone. And if they asked me, I'd tell them he also has a really bad temper and is always throwing tantrums and embarrassing me in front of my friends. But to say he's a D student makes no sense to me, because I know how well he reads and how much he enjoys math and science. My brother may be a handful, but he's a smart handful.

I didn't know about mind-altering drugs that are legal, drugs that are carefully designed to help people with problems bigger than chest congestion . . .

ADD, or attention deficit disorder, causes people to be inattentive and easily distracted. Grant has ADD. Josie's brother Jeff has ADHD, or attention deficit hyperactivity disorder, which means he has the qualities of ADD and is also impulsive and hyperactive. If you know someone who reminds you of either Grant or Jeff, it's possible that he or she has one of these disorders.

ADD and ADHD, like bipolar disorder, are medical disorders caused by chemical problems in the brain. The front part of the brain helps you pay attention, concentrate, organize things, and control impulsive or unacceptable behavior. In people with ADD or ADHD, the front part of the brain may not be able to use its neurotransmitters the way it is supposed to. In this sense, ADD and ADHD are somewhat similar to bipolar disorder—they are all a result of an inability to control feelings, moods, and behaviors.

Even though people with ADD/ADHD (as these disorders are also called) are often very intelligent and creative, and usually have the desire to be good students and workers, their impulsive behavior and difficulty paying attention interfere. Unfortunately, teachers, parents, and friends often

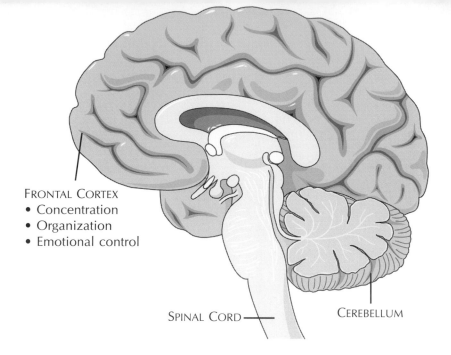

FRONTAL CORTEX
• Concentration
• Organization
• Emotional control

SPINAL CORD

CEREBELLUM

Like bipolar disorder, ADD and ADHD are chemical imbalances caused by the neurotransmitters (message-senders) in the frontal cortex of the brain.

can only see that the person is "misbehaving" or acting "different," and may not be able to tell exactly what is wrong.

Up to 20 percent of the population may have ADD/ADHD. It is the number-one childhood medical disorder in the United States, and experts believe more than 2 million children suffer from it. It is ten times more common in boys than in girls.

Symptoms of hyperactivity in those diagnosed with ADHD may include excessive running or climbing in young children, or extremely restless and fidgety behavior in older children and teens. In contrast to the typical high level of activity in children, hyperactivity is haphazard—

44

Characteristics of ADD/ADHD include an inability to concentrate on one thing for an extended period of time. Many teens with ADD/ADHD have a hard time concentrating in class.

it has no goal. Someone who has ADD/ADHD often shows several of the following characteristics:

- Has difficulty organizing work and gives the impression he or she has not heard instructions
- Is easily distracted
- Makes careless, impulsive errors
- Frequently calls out in the classroom at inappropriate times
- Has a hard time waiting for his or her turn in group situations
- Is unable to concentrate on one thing, such as a game, for extended periods of time

45

46 Without proper treatment, children like Josie's brother and teens like Grant may fall behind in schoolwork, and their friendships may suffer because of inconsiderate behavior stemming from the ADD or ADHD. Negative feelings about themselves can surface when they are repeatedly criticized or punished by teachers and family who do not understand their problem.

For most people with ADD or ADHD, treatment begins with medication. The medication treatment is often multimodal. This means it uses a combination of things to help a person with ADD/ADHD to focus attention and concentrate; to minimize impulsive and hyperactive behavior; and to deal with the emotional, social, behavioral, and educational problems that are symptomatic of ADD and ADHD.

The most common medications used to treat ADD/ADHD are the stimulants Ritalin, Dexedrine, and Cylert. They address areas of attention and concentration, and help minimize hyperactivity. These are successful for between 70 and 75 percent of people diagnosed with ADD or ADHD. Grant's wandering attention during school was significantly minimized when he began taking a stimulant for his ADD. However, for some people, more help is needed.

Josie (Part 2)

When Jeff started taking medication for his ADHD, the Ritalin was supposed to help him concentrate better at school. He took two pills each day, one at breakfast and one at lunch. After a few weeks, his teacher called my parents and had them come in for a conference. For the first time I could ever remember, they came home smiling. Apparently, Jeff was behaving like a completely different student—he was interested in what the class was doing and he rarely spoke out of turn. All of his old disruptive habits—singing jingles from TV commercials, shaking his leg, swinging his foot, tapping his fingers, or just plain squirming and wiggling in his chair—had for the most part completely vanished. Everybody was totally thrilled.

I thought this was all very weird, because to me, Jeff didn't seem like a different brother at all. I was still worried, because I knew that other kids were still giving him a hard time on the bus every afternoon, calling him "Spaz" and telling him he was stupid. They always stopped when I got on, but Jeff was usually crying by then. Even though he never said anything about it, I knew this really made him feel terrible. One night, when I told him I'd rather watch a different TV show than the one he wanted to watch, he threw himself down on the

48 *floor and screamed and kicked until I left the room. It didn't seem to me like he was eating very much, either. And lots of nights he refused to talk to me at all—he would just sit in his room doing nothing, clamping his hands over his ears whenever I went in.*

If this was an improvement, I just couldn't see it. It was great that Jeff was doing better in school, but what about all this?

Like Jeff, many people with ADHD also suffer from low self-esteem and depression as a result of living with the disorder. Although stimulants such as Ritalin often produce positive results very quickly , other social problems—such as Jeff's difficulties with a few inconsiderate children and teens on the school bus—usually linger quite a bit longer. Understandably, they often feel very angry about their situation, and they take it out on the people closest to them. Like Josie, these people often end up bearing the brunt of the frustrations ADD and ADHD can cause. Sometimes lithium is prescribed for children who have been diagnosed with ADD or ADHD as a stabilizing companion to focus-enhancing medications such as Ritalin. The decision to give lithium to children is somewhat controversial. According to studies at Ohio

Lithium can help stabilize ADD/ADHD and ease some of the frustrations these disorders cause.

State University and Brown University, children under the age of twelve who are given lithium for behavioral and mood disorders are likely to experience central nervous system difficulties. Complications may include drowsiness, confusion, impaired coordination, hand tremors, nausea, and vomiting.

While these difficulties have been seen in only half of the children who are given lithium, it is clear that the medication should be prescribed for children with extreme caution. For example, it would be of utmost importance in the case of Josie's brother that she and her parents be sure that the physician who recommended a lithium medication for Jeff has had experience in using it

50 | to treat psychiatric illnesses in other children and teens. Josie and her parents should feel completely free to ask the doctor to explain all of the reasons for putting Jeff on lithium, what specific benefits it would provide, all of its potentially negative side effects or dangers, and what, if any, treatment alternatives exist.

CHAPTER 4

Alternatives to Lithium

*A*lthough medication can be quite effective for some children, teens, and adults, it is not necessarily the answer for all individuals. In fact, because the side effects of taking lithium—weight gain, nausea, feeling "out of it"—are so difficult to manage, about 30 percent of all people who start taking lithium stop without consulting their doctor. Stopping treatment due to unbearable side effects is by far the most common reason cited by doctors for lithium's ineffectiveness.

Two other medications fall into the mood stabilizer category with lithium, including carbamazepine and valproate. These were originally used as anticonvulsant medicines to treat epilepsy and other

52 | sources of seizure. Carbamazepine and valproate give patients a choice apart from lithium, but it is a narrow choice. The side effects of these drugs are similar to but even more intense than those of lithium.

Recently, there has been an increase in research and interest in the possible treatment of bipolar illness, ADD/ADHD, and other mood and behavior disorders without medication. One of the more interesting alternatives is a process called repeated transcranial magnetic stimulation of the brain. This involves placing a magnet shaped like the number eight over the front left of the brain and then directing a rapidly fluctuating series of magnetic fields into the skull. By doing this, doctors can stimulate the brain with electrical discharge. Patients are awake during this whole process, able to describe what they are feeling. Although these tests are still in very early stages, researchers have found that this procedure is about 70 percent effective in stabilizing moods and does not damage brain function.

The "Talking Cure"

Some people with bipolar disorder have found relief and recovery by combining less invasive medications like Prozac with an intensive schedule of psychiatric therapy.

In therapy, either in a group setting or one-on-one, people suffering from mood disorders are given the opportunity to talk with professional counselors about the specific details of their feelings. Memories, relationships with loved ones, daily struggles, and recurring fears or anxieties are topics of conversation to explore. A trained professional can help a person with these sorts of problems.

It is often easier to talk honestly and openly about these issues with someone who is not a friend or family member. By actually speaking about the kinds of feelings that might otherwise stay bottled up inside, a mood-disordered person can often achieve a clearer perspective on the patterns and causes of her or his difficulties.

Clearly, just as drug therapy is not a surefire cure-all for everyone, talk therapy is not necessarily a solution for everyone with a mood disorder. But most people can benefit greatly from spending at least a few months in therapy.

In the end, the decision to begin lithium treatment should always be made carefully and deliberately, considering the whole range of options and alternatives. You can do a lot to help make your or your loved one's choice the right one.

Psychotherapy, in a group setting or one-on-one, can help you understand your feelings.

You're Not Alone

If the kinds of problems discussed in this book are interfering with school and your relationships with family and friends, it's a good idea to seek help right away. These agencies and organizations listed in Where to Go for Help can supply you with more information on lithium and other mood stabilizers, bipolar disorder and other mood disorders, and ADD/ADHD. They can also put you in touch with a variety of support groups and services in your city or town.

Glossary

antidepressant A drug that stimulates chemicals in the brain, prescribed for people suffering from depression.

attention deficit disorder (ADD) A disorder caused by chemical imbalances in the brain that interferes with attention span and concentration.

attention deficit hyperactivity disorder (ADHD) A disorder that causes people to be inattentive, and easily distracted, and unable to control impulsive or unacceptable behavior.

barbiturate A drug that helps to calm people who are anxious or hysterical.

bipolar disorder An ongoing mood disorder that involves marked changes in

a person's behavior between happiness
and depression.

depression A disorder marked by sadness, difficulty in thinking and concentration, and trouble sleeping.

endorphins Chemicals in the brain stimulated by physical activity that act as natural antidepressants.

genetic Referring to biological traits passed on from parents.

hyperactivity Difficulty controlling moods and feelings.

low self-esteem Negative thoughts about oneself.

mania Extremely high-strung and energetic behavior.

neurotransmitters Chemical messengers sent from the brain that carry signals to nerve cells and affect mood.

stimulants Medications such as Ritalin, Dexedrine, and Cylert that increase the heart rate and are used for treating hyperactivity.

Where to Go For Help

These agencies and organizations can supply you with more information on lithium and other mood stabilizers, bipolar disorder and other mood disorders, and ADD/ADHD. They can also put you in touch with a variety of support groups and services in your city or town.

American Academy of Psychotherapists
   (AAP)
P.O. Box 607
Decatur, GA 30031
(404) 299-6336

American Counseling Association
5999 Stevenson Avenue

Alexandria, VA 22313
(703) 823-9800

Children and Adults with Attention
    Deficit/Hyperactivity Disorder (CHAAD)
499 Northwest 70th Avenue, Suite 101
Plantation, FL   33317
(800) 233-4050

Harbor of Refuge
Peer to Peer Support for People with
    Bipolar Illness and the People Who
    Care About Them
http://www.harbor-of-refuge.org/

Learning Disabilities Association of
    America (LDA)
4156 Library Road
Pittsburgh, PA   15234
(412) 341-1515

The Lithium Information Center
Dean Foundation for Health, Research,
    and Education
2711 Allen Boulevard
Middleton, WI 53562
(608) 827-2390

Mental Health Crisis Hotline
(800) 222-8220

60 | Mental Health Information Center
National Mental Health Association
1021 Prince Street
Alexandria, VA 22314-2971
(800) 969-6642

National Depressive and Manic-Depressive Association (NDMD)
730 North Franklin Street, Suite 501
Chicago, IL   60610-3526
(800) 826-3632

Suicide Prevention Hotline
(800) 227-8922

In Canada:

Canadian Mental Health Association
2610 Yonge Street
Toronto, Ontario M45 223
(416) 484-7750

CHAAD Canada
1376 Bank Street
Ottawa, ON   K1H 1B2
(613) 731-1207

For Further Reading

Alexander-Roberts, Colleen. *ADHD and Teens: A Parent's Guide to Making It Through the Tough Years*. Dallas: Taylor Publishing, 1995.

Breggin, Peter R. *Toxic Psychiatry*. New York: St. Martin's Press, 1991.

Garland, E. Jane. *Depression Is the Pits, But I'm Getting Better: A Guide for Adolescents*. Washington, DC: Magination, 1997.

Kaufman, Gershen, and Lev Raphael. *Stick Up for Yourself!: Every Kid's Guide to Personal Power and Positive Self-Esteem*. Minneapolis: Free Spirit Publishing, 1990.

Miklowitz, David J., Michael J. Goldstein,

62

and Lyman C. Wynne. *Bipolar Disorder: A Family-Focused Treatment Approach.* New York: Guilford Press, 1997.

Miller, Susan B. *When Parents Have Problems: A Book for Teens and Older Children with an Abusive, Alcoholic, or Mentally Ill Parent.* New York: Charles C. Thomas Publishing, 1995.

Roseen, Theodore E., and Gail B. Stewart. *Teens and Depression.* San Diego: Lucent Books, 1998.

Salzman, Bernard. *The Handbook of Psychiatric Drugs: A Consumer's Guide, Second Edition.* New York: Henry Holt, 1996.

Index

About the Author

Daniel Eshom is an editor and writer. He lives in New York City.

Photo Credits

Cover, pp. 2, 17, 20, 27, 29, 31, 45, 49, 54 by Les Mills; p. 11 by Ira Fox; p. 18 Ethan Zindler; pp. 15, 32, 37 by © Custom Medical Stock Photo; p. 16 © FPG International.